A Blue-Collar Man
The Importance of America's Hard-Working People

by

Emanuel Zamir

RoseDog 🐾 Books

PITTSBURGH, PENNSYLVANIA 15222

The contents of this work including, but not limited to, the accuracy of events, people, and places depicted; opinions expressed; permission to use previously published materials included; and any advice given or actions advocated are solely the responsibility of the author, who assumes all liability for said work and indemnifies the publisher against any claims stemming from publication of the work.

HD
8038
.A1
Z26
2011

RoseDog Books
701 Smithfield Street
Pittsburgh, PA 15222
Visit our website at *www.rosedogbookstore.com*

ISBN: 978-1-4349-8384-8
eISBN: 978-1-4349-4632-4

Contents

Prologue: **Center of Planet Earth: The Blue-Collar Worker** v

Chapter One: **Our World's Foundation: The Common Worker** 1

Chapter Two: **Teaming Up with the Core of Labor** 4

Chapter Three: **Absolute Dedication** 8

Chapter Four: **Owners and Management Relating to the Workforce**....14

Chapter Five: **Maintaining Long-Term Workforce Continuum** 18

Prologue

Center of Planet Earth:
The Blue-Collar Worker

Over the centuries, since humans walked on Earth, the hierarchy in most civilizations was constructed in a way which put the simple-working people at the bottom of the society ladder. For thousands of years, for the most part, the simple workers were always tasked with all the hard labor. *The blue-collar worker has done it all:* from building multiple structures, cabins, houses, buildings for practicing religion, palaces, and more.

When land was needed to be cleared for construction or creating walking paths and roads, there stood the blue-collar workers, putting their shoulders to the wheel and completing all the tasks.

At any given time in history, the core of the planet Earth and the key force behind most major accomplishments have been the common worker. Without the great efforts of the simple worker, the world would not function at all. All the technology and inventions in the world would be meaningless, unless materialized by the workers. Throughout the history of the world, governments, scientists, and all heavy thinkers played a major role in our society; however, without the common worker, how would the world exist? Without all the simple and heavy labor, commerce, industry, trade, and import and export of important goods would not happen. This book acknowledges the blue-collar workers and puts them in a bright spotlight to be appreciated by all.

Chapter One

Our World's Foundation: The Common Worker

The wonders of the world—those still existing and the ones that are in ruins, along with modern skyscrapers and other enormous constructions around the world—are testimonies to one common factor called "The Blue-Collar Worker."

A large part of humanity is made up of the average and simple worker, who is at the center of everything in life, from the very simple products made to giant projects such as buildings, bridges, tunnels, and the like.

These are the people who make commerce, business, projects, and many chores happen. It is a fact that each country in the world is run by governments and influential businesses. Nevertheless, all the commands and directions on Earth would do no good, unless they are materialized by the common worker, the one who makes things happen. The common worker, for the most part, is a hard-working person, usually not appreciated enough, yet has the mentality to accomplish any task, no matter how difficult or tedious it may be.

Acknowledging the common worker, I would have to start with the medical team first. Starting with the nurses who work each day to near exhaustion to heal people and save lives, together with the doctors and other medical personnel. There is never enough that could be said to adequately show them the appreciation they deserve.

Praising the firefighters is quite easy, as we could not thank them enough for risking their lives every minute they are out on the job, saving lives and reducing major disasters into a minimum damage possible. We are looking at the absolute heroes in society, especially where most of them are volunteers.

We are all familiar with the Wild West era, where chaos ruled in America and no person was safe. You can definitely see the major contribution law enforcement personnel are providing to society while risking their lives daily. It is very simple. Without order, there is absolute chaos, which affects people of all walks of life, businesses, the economy, and life.

Did you ever try spending years of your life underground? There, they are the unseen workers who labor under the face of the earth. They are the miners who you only hear about when a mine disaster strikes.

Considering that mining is a great part of life in the entire world, these workers must be appreciated much more for risking their lives each moment they spend under the earth's crust, so the rest of us could live comfortably.

The fact is that mining is a very active part of life today all around the globe. There is coal mining for generating power and electricity, along with zinc, gold, copper, and multitude of other minerals that are mined and utilized in daily life.

For example, a personal computer is made of dozens of minerals that are mined. Without these minerals, what would life be? What separates humans from the animals on Earth is the use of the brain and knowledge to make the proper decisions in life.

Over the centuries, the one factor that kept humans progressing was education. Do we dare imagine what would this world be without education? Back to cave men and the dark ages is where it would be. Teachers of all levels of education, from those teaching pre-kindergarten children to teachers of high education, must be greatly acknowledged for their enormous contribution to society.

I would now mention the workers who perform a very important work, much more important than people perceive. They are the trash collectors, sewer workers, and landfill workers.

Simply imagine these workers were non-existent. It is easy to figure out the spread of rats, variety of vermin, and other disease-causing agents this situation would cause. I believe this paints a clearer picture of the great importance of sanitation workers.

The reason humans are not still hunters and gatherers, is the farmer. Included are all types of farmers: the ones who provide grain for bread, those who provide fruits and vegetables, and those providing meat. Just imagine needing to hunt and gather food for living.

At this point, I would mention the fisherman, because most of us eat fish and a variety of seafood. These food providers must be highly appreciated.

Would you not acknowledge the importance of all construction workers? This includes workers who build houses, roads, bridges, tunnels, schools, and a variety of buildings. Where would society be without them? You must appreciate their daily efforts and the hard work they do without complaining much. They just keep on working and doing what is necessary to accomplish what they set out to do.

Must be mentioned here are plumbers and all groups of electrical tradesmen. These workers have become most necessary in our lives, unless people are willing to go back to fetching water from the well, river, or streams, and light up their homes with candles. Without these groups, there would be no industry whatsoever.

Do people travel? Do they go in and out of airports while traveling by air from city to city and country to country? Of course, they do, all the time. One key component in travel, whether for business or pleasure, vacationing or visiting relatives, is the taxi driver. Most taxi drivers drive for hours each day, taking people to their destinations and thereby completing the travel itinerary for most people, keeping travel flowing all around the globe.

Every society must have an outlet from the grind of daily life and work, in order to keep a decent mental state and feel relaxed and happy. This is where the entertainment people come in, to boost the people's moral and keep life interesting. This was true for hundreds of years, especially in times of wars or recession, where humans needed a spirit lifter and an outlet to keep them in a good frame of mind.

Here are some more hard-working people, those who work long hours in very hard jobs, such as assembly lines for variety of products: cars, soft drinks, milk and other beverages, all types of machinery parts, and much more.

Generally, you don't hear too many complaints from these people. They just bear down and work hard each day of the week, and the net result is production and industry.

It is easy to realize that all types of workers mentioned and many more who were not mentioned are "the common worker." They are indeed "the world foundation" and should always be viewed as such and appreciated.

Chapter Two

Teaming Up with the Core of Labor

Some major elements that became my way of life are total respect, appreciation, and great communication for almost all workers I have been associated with.

It is a fact that no project would be complete without full cooperation from workers of various trades, from a janitor all the way up to a company CEO (chief executive officer).

From the early 1980s to the late 1990s, I was privileged to work for a large nationwide company which dealt with the electronics and electrical field. For nearly half that time span, I had the honor to be a technical specialist for a group of over seventy field engineers and at least a hundred clients, in an area that spread from Maine to North Carolina and from Cape Cod to Ohio.

It was during these years when I came to respect and appreciate workers from all trades, as well as the skill of great communication. Although the electronics and electrical field has been very technical in nature, I never looked at workers from other trades as less than equal persons.

It did not matter if the person I dealt with was a janitor who had the keys to the equipment room where work was being done, an electrician we were working with at the time, a client representative or the owner of the company, and even the CEO of the company.

I treated them all with the same respect, not thinking one was a better person than the other.

Were you ever in a situation where you turned for someone's help? It makes no difference what your stature in society might be. At some point in your life, you needed to ask for some sort of help. It could have been a real small issue, such as asking for directions when you got lost in an unfamiliar area or asking for a bus, train, or flight schedule.

Were you particular or concerned who the person was? I think not. This experience teaches us that any person you may communicate with in any way holds as much importance as any other.

Personally, over the years, I have been in numerous situations where I needed to ask for someone's help, as much as I prefer to solve all matters on my own like most people do.

I may have needed some information, such as the whereabouts of key personnel during repair of critical equipment at a bank, or even regarding building operation procedures, where the only person around was a building maintenance technician and our contact person was away. I had no problem asking the technician and was thankful for the information.

We once had a critical situation where we needed to replace sixty batteries inside electronic-equipment cabinets at an important bank in Washington, DC.

The batteries weighed over one hundred pounds each and needed to be unloaded from a truck that had no lift-gate one at a time, taken to an elevator headed for the fourth floor, and then assembled in tight cabinets.

Our crew consisted of only two people, which meant that we needed some help in this project. We asked for help hauling the batteries from two technicians who were with a different division within our company, after going over battery safety rules. We were very grateful to these technicians for their willingness to provide help.

There was a situation during critical maintenance at a facility which could not afford equipment down time, lest they lose millions of dollars. The equipment at this facility needed to be back online at a specific time, as dictated by the client. We had to put numerous subassemblies back together in a very short time, complete with all wiring connections, startup the equipment, and put it back online.

Because we were shorthanded at the time, we asked for assistance from building electricians, and were grateful for their help. Other situations required access to certain rooms when our contact person was not around, or the need for some special tools or ladders. In the vast majority of these cases, we received assistance from building maintenance people and others. Their help was critical, and for that, we could not thank them enough.

It is a known fact that no person is perfect. There were many projects and jobs that required certain expertise, which included all kinds of tradesmen working together at the same location, and sometimes next to each other for several hours at a time. During these times, it was common to see a variety of behavior, some funny and some not too classy. We took the humor with a grain of salt and completed our work.

Teaming up with the core of labor materialized for me, not only with the client's workers but also within the company I worked for. From the late 1990s to the middle of the 2000s, I worked for a company that was so diversified. It dealt with mostly electrical and electronics fields.

Within the company's workforce, there were electricians, electronics technicians, electrical engineers, electrical estimators, and more. Over the eight years I worked there, we had many joint operations between electronics technicians, electricians, electrical estimators, and electrical engineers.

One of these joint operations was an absolutely astonishing project, due to a client mandated extremely small window, by which the entire project had to be 100 percent completed and tested prior to the move of this company's entire operation from New Jersey to Virginia.

This project displayed a combination of the best teamwork, cooperation, and expertise I have seen in over twenty-five years working in this field. Most workers had to work around the clock with almost no breaks, several items needed to be rebuilt or modified in order to meet specifications, a multitude of wiring needed to be assembled from scratch, and all in a very narrow window.

The project was completed ahead of schedule and some of the crew members witnessed the client's grand opening. The crew who accomplished the near impossible project is what I call "core of labor."

A large TV station in the Northeast experienced a major electrical problem at the worst possible time, when they were broadcasting a very important event. We were called in to identify the problem, provide immediate solution, and provide power to client's equipment as soon as it was possible. I had the privilege to team up with two electricians who were masters of their craft and with two highly knowledgeable electrical engineers to provide the client a solution.

The first phase included a provision of temporary power to the client's computer room without any down time for the work that needed to be done outside normal business hours. This phase was accomplished smoothly and in a timely manner. Thanks again to a complete teamwork. The second phase was a highly engineered electrical design that really showed expertise. This phase was pending the client's approval in consideration of future planning. During the eight years I worked for this company, I always enjoyed the great teamwork with each and every coworker. The bulk of the equipment maintenance was typically performed during odd hours, such as midnight until 6 A.M., with continuous work involving removal of heavy sections, analyzing and reassembling them, and calibrating the entire unit.

I always liked that atmosphere and the great communication we had. We were the "core of labor," and each person possessed great knowledge and completed every assignment we were tasked with.

Our company had a major distributor who provided us with some equipment and material, but mainly with batteries of all sorts, an item that needed replacement on every piece of equipment every three to four years on the average.

This distributor provided us not only with batteries, but also with a labor force on multiple projects. Some of these projects were medium-sized, but quite a few were huge installations.

I can't give enough praise to this distributor, to the owners of that company, and to each worker on their workforce, simply because they spelled "professionalism," and they were most definitely qualified as "core of labor."

Oftentimes, our source of new clients and new projects was the sales force of another good company I worked for earlier, which constantly involved us in all sorts of installations and maintenance projects.

These were real professional salesmen who had overall knowledge of what the equipment could provide the customer with and constantly addressed the customer's needs.

I must say that it was gratifying working with them, and again, there was always teamwork involved here from the first meeting with a client until the project was 100 percent completed.

For over twenty-five years working in the electronics and electrical field, I was truly fortunate to work for professional organizations, but most of all, with professional coworkers. These coworkers ranged from material and parts handlers to electricians, engineers, and my own group.

Chapter Three

Absolute Dedication

There is no better way one could learn than from being thrown right into the hot tub. This phrase existed for many years and I found it to be very true. The year 1981 was when my career in the electronics and electrical field started soaring.

It started with a job interview at a New York diner, conducted by one of the best managers in this field I have ever been associated with, both for personality and great knowledge. The company I started working for had a collection of great minds in the electronics and electrical field.

I can't forget the first lesson I learned starting up electrical equipment the size of a school bus, with a couple of 2000 amperes circuit breakers, huge transformers, and big assemblies.

It is rather funny that earlier that week, a candidate for this job looked at this equipment and said, "This is not for me, man," and proceeded to walk out the door. That same week, another candidate for the job who witnessed the equipment start up, jumped two feet off the ground, as soon as the circuit breaker was energized and then walked out the door. The sheer electrical power of that machine was awesome.

When I started working for this company, there were just the five of us covering the Northeast region: the manager and four field engineers. We had quite a few clients, so we kept busy, as these were the early days of rapidly increasing demand for equipment called UPS (uninterruptible power supply), in an industry that I had the privilege to see grow in great strides over the following twenty-five years.

During this time, I have learned so much about this field and industry, and was always glad to share my knowledge with the newly hired field engineers, which increased in number by leaps and bounds.

Starting in 1981 and for the next several years, the transportation I was using almost on a weekly basis was Eastern Airlines. I would typically take the earliest shuttle flight from New York to Boston, arrive at a client's jobsite, perform the equipment repairs, startup or maintenance, and catch the very last shuttle flight heading back to New York.

Doing this type of work has been described as being a modern day cowboy, which I really enjoyed. The constant travel to clients' jobsites gave me great opportunity to meet lots of people in this field, where a completion of each equipment repair, maintenance, or startup was rewarding.

For me, this emphasized the fact that because I liked my work and got along with people, I had a good sense of accomplishment, not only a sense of being monetarily rewarded.

California was the company's hub for engineering and manufacturing. The travel to California was associated with training on new equipment, as well as conferences with the equipment design engineers, which is what I loved the most for the following reasons: I could pick the engineer's brain on many design concepts, I brought with me a list of recommended modifications such as adding some indicators and monitoring circuits, and also provided feedback from the field, which aided in equipment upgrades and modifications.

Modifications and upgrades on the equipment were ongoing practices, as the equipment performance and reliability kept improving. It was during the engineering conferences and conversations with the design engineers that I acquired most of my knowledge of design concepts and troubleshooting methods, knowledge I put to use daily and was more than happy to share with many field engineers over the years.

The number of clients increased dramatically over the next few years, which necessitated hiring many field engineers. The increase in labor force required on-the-job training and technical support, in order to bring all the new technicians up to par.

For me, this was a starting point where I could really make a difference, both for our company and the clients. I have used every bit of my knowledge and experience to aid the field engineers and clients and took the role of technical support very seriously, as if our company was my own.

At times, trusting that equipment wiring done by installing electricians was correct, prior to equipment startup, have caused mini fires, several blown components, and some injuries. The field we were engaged in was fairly dangerous and always required total awareness and concentration.

Over the years, the one aspect that I adhered to real well was the follow-up, in several ways: follow-up with field engineers after the completion of assignment and follow-up with clients to ensure their operation is running smoothly and ensure they are happy with our service.

I always followed up, looking at blue prints and technical documents at home after each repair, to fully understand each and every circuit associated with the problem and to always find the cause of the fault, not just the effect. I always noticed that the majority of field engineers are content with repairing the effects of a problem and not looking for the cause, let alone looking at blue prints, which usually caused reoccurring problems.

It was in 1988 when the UPS industry was booming, and with it, the expansion of technical support, both for area coverage and number of field engineers. This equipment was used by just about every important outfit under the sun: banks, hospitals, investment firms, insurance companies, transportation departments, government buildings, airports, and even jail houses.

The area of coverage in the technical support aspect, both to field engineers and clients alike, stretched from Maine to the North Carolina border and from Massachusetts to the Ohio border. The number of field engineers I assisted on a twenty-four-hour basis was over seventy, and the number of clients was over one hundred; yet, I took my work in stride and gladly addressed each and every situation with great patience.

It was very common for me to receive a phone call, mostly from field engineers and at times directly from clients, between 2 A.M. and 4 A.M. on any given day, seeking help to restore the equipment to a good working order.

All I did, time and time again, is to assist each and every person, and with eyes half closed, dug into blueprints to get a resolution to the situation. At times, the problem could not be resolved over the phone, which necessitated a trip to the jobsite, either driving to the equipment location that same day or flying out there the following day.

One thing we made sure was for the equipment to be running in good order before we left the client's jobsite, which we worked very hard to ensure.

From my point of view, the field engineers who were battling equipment problems in the middle of the night, many times out in nowhere, must get all the help they could in order to get a resolution and go home to their families; as far as I was concerned, it was my job to see to it! That is why in all the years I have worked as a technical specialist, I spared no effort to help each and every person in every way I could. It has always been my mentality.

Starting in 1989, I took on a bigger role as a regional technical specialist, where I needed to provide technical support to more field engineers and more clients along the Northeast region. Needless to say, the phone calls at the early hours of the morning increased, along with the travel volume to jobsites, as well as on-the-job training. I worked with a group which had some very bright minds in the electronics and electrical field.

I took only one approach, that any technical assistance is my responsibility, and expanded my role by writing technical documents such as calibration manuals, troubleshooting tips, safety tips, and listings of required equipment modifications. I also obtained all manuals pertaining to equipment that each field engineer was trained on and distributed them. In addition to that, I was in charge of ensuring timely calibration of test equipment for each person and always kept looking for the latest and greatest in test equipment available on the market, which could have made our job easier.

I believe that in a way, I helped redefine technical support using one key element, *care*.

I especially liked going to jobsites for major startups which had many pieces of equipment, at times, over a dozen just in one location, a startup that took a few months to complete.

The most interesting phase of the startup was the equipment final testing, which required rigorous tests on each piece of equipment, to include what we used to call "baby sitting" the equipment. These tests were performed with all sorts of test equipment hooked up to the system under test.

When the tests were completed and passed with flying colors, you could feel a sense of accomplishment. Of course, some felt a sense of "we are finally going home."

There is an element of comedy in almost every environment, and our field was no exception. It was at a large bank in New York, where several pieces of equipment were in the installation phase.

The installing electricians had a strange sense of humor. They brought with them a variety of colored paper, ribbons, twigs, branches, balloons, and other items, and proceeded to decorate each piece of equipment, as if it were Macy's Thanksgiving parade.

Another episode happened at a large facility in Connecticut during major equipment maintenance. While maintaining the equipment, one technician had his tools scattered around one unit which was turned off. As he got up picking up a tool from the floor, his back pocket caught the handle of a circuit breaker and energized it, resulting in several units shutting down.

A large telecommunications company in New York had a huge electrical system, which was actually a UPS prototype. Each of the three units in that system was as long as a semi-trailer, with thousands of components and a strange temperament.

For a long while, this system had a strange habit of shutting down on Friday evenings with intermittent problems, an event that would ruin a technician's weekend just trying to identify the cause.

There was one technician assigned to that particular jobsite. Out of frustration with the system's problems, he once proceeded to talk to the machine and beg it not to go down. When talking to the machine failed him, he started crying to the machine, begging it not to go down.

At that same location, one of the three units started acting up and was shutting down every now and then. Among the client's maintenance crew was an electrician who have been bragging for a while that he was a soldier in a commando unit.

One evening while he was taking some readings of that unit with two other electricians, a component inside the unit ruptured, creating a loud noise. That commando guy was the first to run out of the room with his hands on his head.

We had quite a few characters on our workforce, such as one technician who was assigned a service call. The next morning, he was going to take care of his assignment. He walked into the equipment room where the customer was waiting for him. Our technician was dressed in overalls and without a shirt, had boots on, a straw hat, and a pipe in his mouth. It might have seemed unprofessional, but it was funny.

When you ignore a good technical advice because you are cheap, something will happen. I once received a call from a client at Upstate New York to have one of his machines repaired. Entering the equipment room, I noticed that a battery system in the adjacent room had large number of battery posts covered with chunks of green corrosive deposits.

I immediately pointed out to the customer that he was looking at an accident waiting to happen, and the sooner the situation is corrected, the better. The client's reply was, "You don't need to worry about this system. Just fix the unit in the next room."

About a week later, during a utility power outage, several batteries exploded, covering the entire floor with acid.

In 1998, I started working for a company that was basically an electrical engineering and service outfit but was incredibly diversified, as it encompassed just about everything associated with the electronics and electrical field, and even included software design.

I worked for this company for eight years, witnessing a tremendous growth of nearly every aspect of the company. This outfit had some of the best minds in their particular trade: electricians, engineers, electronics technicians, computer specialists, and software personnel.

The interesting part about working for this company was our particular group, which started with several people and had no clients to begin with.

At the beginning, our group started knocking on doors, doing lots of cold-calling type sales, until we acquired several clients and amazingly expanded our client base to show decent profit in less than a year.

As the number of our clients increased, we hired more field engineers and acquired even more clients, as we were involved in all sorts of installations and major projects.

I particularly liked working in that atmosphere and with top professionals, and the fact that we started out with almost nothing but slowly built our client base and the group's profit along the way.

Compared to previous years when I was working for a big company with lots of resources, in this company, *we were the resources* and had to build our business, brick by brick, which was very gratifying.

In this line of work, there were many projects and jobs that required working into the night, which did not really bothered us, for we were dedicated and glad to do our work.

I always appreciated and respected every person I was associated with: the warehouse material handlers, material coordinators, tool rental personnel, electricians, office personnel, my own group of field engineers, electrical engineers, computer experts, managers, and all the way up to the company's owner.

I viewed our clients as friends and family members, and always treated them as such. The relationship between our group and each and every client was great, no matter how small or large a business they would bring.

The key to our success was *great teamwork* and terrific communication with each other, on every project and assignment we took on. The level of expertise, knowledge, and intelligence within this group was extremely high, coupled with *hard work and no complaints* mentality.

This has been a great group that accomplished everything it set out to do, including what seemed to be the impossible.

You quite often find field engineers in many companies who refuse to do a job they deem menial. Our group would have none of that attitude. We would have designed a circuit or a piece of equipment for a specific job one day, hauled dozens of heavy batteries the following day, and attended a client's technical- conference the day after.

This mentality, of *do what it takes to build and develop our business*, is very unique in any industry and the key word there was *care*. Other elements that are lost on other companies are: work quality, precision, great care of a client, and absolute determination. When you build a company or a service group of any kind, use this particular group as a model, and you are assured of one thing: *great success*.

Chapter Four

Owners and Management Relating to the Workforce

When you live in a castle that is absolutely immaculate outside as well as inside, where the carpeting, stairs, and walls are all plush, you ensure it is maintained that way for many years to come.

This concept is the root of sound business by business owners and management below them in a typical enterprise. Capitalism, which many businesses in the world adheres to, compared to other systems, is still the better system.

In this system, the ultimate goal is maximum profitability, and to achieve this goal, there is a natural mass which starts from the CEO and major stock holders at the top, funnels through management, and finally rests on the shoulders of the common workforce.

For the most part, over many generations, this has been a normal practice and a way of life, most everywhere throughout the free world enterprise.

All players in the enterprise starting from the CEO and down the chain of command are following these steps, guided by the nature of a system put in front of them. There are better ways to maximize profitability and take better care of the workforce at the same time.

There are quite a few successful businesses in the world that walk in a little different path.

There are small businesses and family owned businesses around the globe that relate to the workforce in a different way.

Aside from certain fringe benefits that are generally incorporated everywhere, these unique businesses employ a strategy which provides additional benefits to the workforce and has a mentality that states: "The common workforce is the key to our success."

Relating to the common worker in a different way than customary revealed itself at a company I worked for from 1981 to 1997. For quite a few years, the field engineer in this company was treated almost as a family member by company owners and upper management.

When they claimed to have an open-door policy, it meant exactly that. Several suggestions or ideas brought to their attention were at least considered, and often enough implemented, when they made good business sense, while improving the workers' working conditions.

Field engineers received some meal allowance while working on the field, and also some bonuses when business was real good. In addition to that, there were district and regional meetings each quarter year, where upper management ordered some nice catering and addressed issues at the company's headquarters, which made us feel good and certainly as integral part of the company.

This company realized the importance of each workforce member, the field engineers. They understood that the only way to treat them is as an integral part of the company. This was acknowledged and very much appreciated by the workforce, which resulted in hard work, efficiency, and great output from the field engineers.

Similarly, overseas and right here in the United States of America, there are companies that relate to the common worker as the foundation and the cause for good business and enterprise success.

They treat them with respect and make them feel they are valuable to the company. They incorporate company values and discipline, hand in hand, with empowering the worker and maintaining guidelines and control in order to follow protocol.

Several ways could make a common worker become more valuable, more productive, and a great asset to a company—merits that would enhance profitability and at the same time create a happy and devoted employee, sometimes for many years.

Money alone is not a long-term solution; hence, a raise here and there is good, but it only goes so far as a motivational force that is needed. Making the workers feel very valuable and key contributors to the company's success, by empowering them and getting them to feel as difference makers in the company, that every action they take has direct impact on the direction the business will take.

I once managed an assembly line in the Northeast region. It employed some eighteen workers, whom I trained for a couple of weeks and assembled a team of good workers. Increasing client orders necessitated some off-hours work on the assembly line to complete orders which needed to be ready in a relatively short time.

I had asked each assembly line worker to work the upcoming Saturday, on a short notice. I had no idea how many workers would actually show up and I did not expect half of them to comply. To my surprise, each and every person showed up that Saturday and turned in some great work.

I attributed that turnout to the way I related to each worker, with great respect, empowering them, and making them feel that each minute they spent laboring on the assembly line was a minute of creativity for their own company and was highly appreciated.

As many companies that better relate to the common worker, there are quite a few companies that do not treat their workforce as a major part of the enterprise.

Over the years, you kept on hearing about numerous companies that exploit their workforce and treat them harshly. These companies eventually go out of business in a short time.

Running a good and efficient enterprise and relating to the common worker favorably at the same time doesn't just happen. It takes a certain mentality and a frame of mind of ownership and by upper management to make it happen. Companies that follow this path as a rule experience tremendous gains and stand on solid foundation.

It is rather easy to distinguish between a company that relates to its workforce very well and companies that do not. You can see it on the workers' faces, their general attitude when beginning a day's work, during work, and as they leave the facility.

Another benefit that comes from a real happy and devoted workforce is a solid and improved business, a benefit which extends to the client.

I recently had car trouble which required an emergency repair. The repair shop I normally used was booked solid that afternoon. My contact at the shop made immediate arrangement with another car repair outfit and also arranged for a rental car for me, where the rental car company sent a driver to pick me up from the repair shop and drive me to the car rental facility.

The outfit repairing my car was the classiest I have seen in a long time, as you could see it all around, from the cleanliness of the building inside and outside, cleanliness of the repair shop, and the neat uniforms the mechanics wore, to the nice customer service, offering the clients coffee and soft drinks.

I picked up my car from the repair shop in about twenty-four hours from the time I brought it in. The repair and some additional maintenance that was required were done professionally. That is what I call *great service* and it is the extension of upper management mentality at both car repair shops.

When workers perform their tasks at a company that takes good care of them and relates to them real well, they show a bounce in their step, eagerness to do the job right and with high quality, and show they care about what they are doing.

Opposite this scenario, where management does not treat the workforce that well, you will find workers who do not show they care about the task at hand, as well as the mentality that they only work specified amount of hours in a day and will get paid at the end of the week.

All they are worried about is not to make bad mistakes during their work and collecting their pay check. This kind of attitude can backfire on an organization and lead to an unsuccessful business.

There are two sides to every coin, just like the two opposite directions a business could take. I am referring to the company's upper management relating to the workforce. Taking good care of the common worker is absolutely necessary in order to maintain successful business across the board.

The other side of the coin, providing too many benefits and bonuses to the common worker, could backfire and bankrupt a company.

I worked for a large company that owned hundreds of subsidiaries at the time. One of the subsidiaries had numerous employees and was extremely successful, because the market they catered to had tremendous demand for the product they manufactured and serviced all over the Northeast region, for several years.

The upper management of this outfit started handing out large bonuses and paid double and triple time the hourly rates for off-hour labor. In less than a year, the main company had to bail this outfit out of bankruptcy and made significant changes.

One huge lesson to learn from that situation is that taking great care of the workforce is essential, but it needs to be done with much thought in order to keep the company healthy and strong.

The way the owners and management of a company relate to the workforce determines the health of that company and its long-term success or failure in a very competitive business world.

Chapter Five

Maintaining Long-Term Workforce Continuum

You must wonder why certain companies exist for a hundred years or more, while many companies would not even last for several years.

There are several reasons for this phenomenon. One huge reason is family ownership, which continues from one generation to the next, as this type of business thrives on quality of product, quality of workmanship, and relating to the common workers as if they were family members.

The gains of a company could be tremendous when the entire operation, from the company owners to the very last common worker in the shipping department, is run with good relationship which elevates the all-around morale and creates happy atmosphere.

The positive results of an operation which follows this direction for many years are evident. The goal of each and every company should be *holding on to good workers* for as long as possible, in order to maintain a solid business that will continue to thrive and grow.

This is especially true because of the massive training the company provided to these workers and the experience and knowledge acquired by the workforce, along with specific skills and work ethics they mastered at the company.

Not holding onto these very important workers creates a setback to the company because new workers are required, and when they are found, they need training.

An adage, "Good work is hard to find," is absolutely true. There are many workers in the marketplace encompassing variety of trades, but there are only a handful of real good workers. The definition of a good worker lies in several categories: conscientious person, hard worker who follows instructions well, an employee who really cares about his production and precision of workmanship, and a worker who sees a complete picture of the job which he or she is a small part of.

It takes many years and lots of effort to develop a good worker in any industry. The first and most obvious step is good training, which is followed by stressing to the worker a good mentality regarding the entire operation and getting the employee to see the whole picture of production in general, because that worker is a potential future manager.

Another extremely important developmental tool for a good worker is creating an atmosphere where the worker is self-motivated. Just motivating the worker in different ways, although very important, works for a little while. Getting a person to be self-motivated as a large part of it comes from within the person. The self-motivation lasts for many years to come.

Working for many outfits throughout my career, I can tell with high degree of accuracy that I really know about developing a good worker simply because *I have been one* everywhere I worked. I developed into a real good worker at a company I worked for, for a good seventeen years.

This company, from the CEO to upper management, to regional management and coworkers, knew exactly what it takes to develop good workforce and they kept on turning average workers into good workers.

When I started working for this great company, I already possessed the hard worker's mentality and I also liked working with people. Management and coworkers were always very helpful in conveying work ethics and technical knowledge, without worrying about jeopardizing their own position in the company, as often happens in various companies where many workers are too worried about being replaced by others.

At the beginning, we had but a handful of field engineers covering the Northeast territory, as it became easy for me to recognize and see the whole picture of what the company is all about, exactly what they are trying to accomplish and how they go about it. There was a sense of being part of a family for the most part, where people always helped each other.

Working for this company at the regional and district levels, there always seem to be an atmosphere of fairness, care, and great pride. As the number of clients increased and consequently so did our workforce, there was more to give and more to contribute, such as teaching and training the newcomers and seeing the work-family grow and expand the business.

We used to take turns at being on call after regular business hours in providing support to clients in the entire region and always took it in stride.

There were quite a few field engineers who stayed with the company for many years, where an average worker in most fields typically stayed in a company for a couple of years. I could definitely tell that for the most part, a majority of our workforce felt happy and proud to perform their tasks, and they generally felt the company's upper management took care of them.

The regional-district meetings that were typically held four times a year, where an upper management person would fly in from the west coast for the purpose, were lots of fun and useful time for discussions.

The good attitude of our workforce in the company extended to our clients, which created even a better atmosphere all around. At that point, many clients were treating us as family members, acknowledging our excellent work ethics and the great care we took in servicing the critical equipment in their facility.

This company developed the good worker methodically, patiently, and with a good personal skill. It wasn't only the technical training of the workforce that was important, but the mentality that the client is the core of business and the workers need to be taken care of, so they may concentrate on doing their job in the most efficient way possible.

Companies really ought to follow the example set by this company, simply because this system worked for many years and resulted in a successful company for several decades. Companies may also want to rethink the entire process and procedure regarding development of their workforce and incorporate all changes needed for the sake of the company's growth and prosperity.

The starting point in developing a good worker is hiring the person, assessing the worker's mentality and frame of mind regarding an overall picture of the company's expectations, how the person relates to this most important subject, and not hiring a worker who just use work experience as a parameter.

Once the workers have been hired according to these merits, the following step would be specific training, not only job related training but attitude training in relation to how the workers view their role in the company's growth. The next step would be more specific, in the area of the workers' work ethics, production, accuracy, quality of work, and above all, being conscientious.

Part of the training must address the company's consumer and have the workforce realize what the end product must look like, for the consumer's maximum satisfaction. This is an extremely important part of training, because the worker must always visualize and realize that every little operation would greatly affect the product condition; after all, how many consumers would buy a poor quality product?

The candidates who successfully passed these training steps are on their way to become good workers for the company and need to maintain all aspects of good work as described above.

As compensation for their great efforts, there is always the wage and basic benefits they collect, such as health insurance, vacation time, sick leave, and so on.

Extra motivational tools that companies which relate to the workforce most favorably use include: bonuses for exceeding quota, bonuses for perfect attendance for a certain time period, profit sharing plan which hinges on extraordinary production, and profit during predetermined time span.

The way a company trains, treats, and motivates the workforce will determine the long-term workforce continuum, which ultimately decides the long-term successes of a company.